W9-DGW-860

Contents

Introduction

A screaming crowd of people pushes toward you. A black limousine pulls up to the curb of the United Nations building where you are standing. The rear side door of the limousine opens. Out steps the president of the United States. Many people in the crowd cheer him. A few angry people shout at him.

You carefully look over the crowd. Suddenly, a man catches your eye. He is moving quickly toward the president. He reaches into his jacket. The hair on the back of your neck stands up. Your hunch about the suspicious-looking man is confirmed: He pulls out a gun.

You shout to your fellow agents. They snap into action, surrounding the president and shoving him to the ground. People in the crowd see the gunman. They panic—but you do not. The man aims his gun at the president. Without a thought for your own life, you leap toward the gunman. You wrestle him to the ground, taking the gun from him. The danger

has passed. You have done your job well. As an agent of the U.S. Secret Service, you have just saved the life of the president of the United States.

For more than one hundred years, the U.S. Secret Service has had the job of protecting the president of the United States. It is an important, exciting, and often very dangerous job. It takes quick thinking and nerves of steel.

Let's take a behind-the-scenes look at the Secret Service and the many vital responsibilities it holds.

Fighting Counterfeiters and Assassins

The Secret Service is a branch of the U.S. Treasury Department. The Secret Service was established on July 5, 1865. It was set up by the government to stop the making of counterfeit, or fake, money. People who make counterfeit money are called counterfeiters, or forgers.

The U.S. federal government did not start printing money until 1862. Before this there was no standard currency for the entire country. There were many different kinds of money being used in the United States. Every state, as well as some banks, printed its own paper money.

After the Civil War (1861–1865), prices for goods were very high. In the South, there were very few jobs available. People needed to know that the little money they had was real.

The U.S. Treasury Department knew that the only way to stop counterfeiting was to go after the forgers.

In 1998, Secret Service agents working with local police, broke up a counterfeiting ring, in Jackson, Mississippi, that had made fifty-five thousand dollars in fake money.

CLASSIFIED INFORMATION

It is believed that by 1865 one-third to one-half of the money in use in the United States was counterfeit.

To do this, the department hired agents who were trained to tell the difference between fake money and real money.

Federal Investigators

Secret Service agents proved themselves excellent criminal investigators. Counterfeiters began to fear these agents. The counterfeiters became wary of the people to whom they sold fake money because the buyers could have been undercover agents. They also had to worry about buying goods with their counterfeit bills.

However, counterfeiting was just one criminal problem the U.S. government needed to solve.

Other federal laws were being broken, too. Mail was being stolen from postal workers. People were stealing federal land. Yet there was no federal police force to combat these crimes. The U.S. government decided that the Secret Service should be responsible for handling these crimes, too.

Protection Duties

At the time of his assassination in 1865, President Abraham Lincoln did not have a full-time bodyguard. The federal government did not provide around-the-clock protection for the president. Presidents were expected to arrange for their own protection. It was only after President William McKinley was assassinated in 1901 that the U.S. Congress ordered the Secret Service to protect the president full time.

Expanded Protection Duties

Over the years, the Secret Service's protection duties grew. In 1908, the Secret Service began protecting the president-elect. The president-elect is the person who wins the November presidential election and waits to take office in January of the following year.

In 1917, Congress passed a law that made threats against the president a federal crime. Congress gave the Secret Service the duty of protecting the president's family. It also gave the agency the power to investigate any threats against the president.

In 1922, the White House Police Force was set up to protect the president's residence and grounds. In 1930, the White House Police Force became a part of the Secret Service. Since 1977, the White House Police Force has been known as the Secret Service Uniform Division.

CLASSIFIED INFORMATION

The Secret Service has about 125 field offices. Most of these offices are located in the United States. The rest of the offices are in foreign countries.

The Secret Service Uniform Division is always dressed for defense when they patrol the grounds of the White House.

In the 1960s, Congress passed laws to protect vice presidents and former presidents. In 1968, presidential candidate Robert F. Kennedy was assassinated. Congress immediately passed a law aimed at protecting presidential and vice presidential candidates.

Secret Service Agents at Work Today

In the early years that the Secret Service protected the president, the agents acted simply as bodyguards. Agents stayed with the president inside his residence, the White House, and whenever he was out in public. Today, the Secret Service follows strict, detailed guidelines for protecting the president and his family. These guidelines are also used for anyone else the Secret Service is ordered to protect.

Meanwhile, the Secret Service's financial crimes division is always on the prowl for counterfeiters, frauds, and Internet crimes.

In the late 1800s, the Secret Service had only about thirty-five agents. Today, the Secret Service employs five thousand people. There are about 2,100 special agents, 1,200 Uniform Division Officers, and about 1,700 other people who work in technical, professional, and administrative support positions.

Protection "Web"

The busy, around-the-world travel schedule of a U.S. president keeps Secret Service agents on their toes. If the president is going on a trip, the Secret Service swings into action by setting up a web of security rules for his protection. Each building that he will visit is carefully studied. The Secret Service agents must locate all the exits and entrances. They have to look for all the possible places an assassin could hide.

The Secret Service never takes a vacation, even when the first family does. When former first lady Hillary Clinton went skiing in 1999, a Secret Service agent followed her every move.

The agents must figure out the best lookout spots for keeping an eye on things. Every inch of the route the president takes by car to his destination is carefully planned. The streets his car takes, the speed at which it drives, how the local police will get involved, and many other issues are planned. Also, agents investigate the people working at the place the president will visit. Who has access to the building? What are the backgrounds of these people? In short, the Secret Service takes full control of the security of the president's trips and public appearances.

Secret Service agents are always on the lookout for danger. These men are a part of the Secret Service's Counter Sniper Division.

>>>

The agents' work gets even more intense on the day the president arrives at his destination. They search the building, and nearby buildings, for bombs and electronic devices, such as hidden cameras and microphones. Sharpshooter agents take position on top of surrounding buildings. They watch the entrance of the building where the president will be, keeping a close eye on who goes in and out. Other agents with binoculars station themselves to watch the crowd, the buildings, and the traffic.

Whenever the president is in public, Secret Service agents are always nearby. Here they run alongside the limousine of President George W. Bush, directly in the line of would-be assassins.

The president rides in an armored limousine. Cars filled with agents lead and follow the president's car. Often, two limousines that look exactly the same ride in the presidential motorcade, or group of cars. Of course, the president is in only one of the limousines. This is done to confuse any would-be assassins. Finally, a van filled with weapons and agents follows this group.

This protective web works because agents are in constant contact with each other. They use wrist-mounted radios as well as earpieces for communicating with one another. Some agents are easy to spot in a crowd. Others hide so that they cannot be seen. Agents are always watching for the sure signs of an assassin. They watch to see if anyone has a hand placed inside a jacket or pants pocket. This could mean that person is reaching for a gun. Agents also watch for people making quick movements toward the president. Even an open window in a nearby building will draw the attention of a Secret Service agent. Nothing about the president's safety is left to chance.

Criminals love using credit cards, especially
when they belong to someone else.

Counterfeiting and Fraud

Tracking down money counterfeiters is still a large
part of the Secret Service's job. However, the nature
of financial crime has changed over the years. Since
credit cards first appeared in the 1950s, criminals
have found ways to use them to commit financial
fraud. Fraud means to trick someone by being

dishonest. Some criminals use people's personal information, such as social security numbers, to apply for, and get, credit cards. Other criminals use machines that make credit cards. These "homemade" credit cards often look just like real credit cards.

Secret Service agents use a variety of methods to catch criminals. Agents use good old-fashioned footwork, by finding forgery operations and setting up "buys." In a buy, agents pretend to be criminals and set up a time and place to buy illegal items the real criminals are selling. When these real criminals show up, they are arrested. The agents also use the Internet to track groups who use the Internet to commit crime.

While the Internet is very helpful to the Secret Service, it also causes them problems. Many criminals have figured out how to make the Internet work for them. Some of these criminals set up fraud and counterfeit operations using Web sites and chat groups. These types of crime are called e-crimes. E-criminals may break into the information system of an on-line retail store or business. The Internet criminals can often steal the credit card information of shoppers who have bought something from that store. They use the stolen credit card numbers to buy expensive things for themselves. Often, these criminals sell the stolen credit card numbers to other criminals.

Identity theft has also become a big problem. Identity theft is when a person's personal information is used to set up fake credit accounts. Then, e-criminals buy items in the person's name.

Not only can e-criminals steal information from innocent Internet users, but they can also break into government data banks and steal or alter important information. The Secret Service is now using sophisticated technology to track these criminals. Nearly two hundred agents are now permanently assigned to the Secret Service's Electronic Crimes Division.

Chapter Two

Secret Service Agent Training

There are many different jobs at the Secret Service. The Secret Service employs lawyers, accountants, chemists, photographers, administrative assistants, and computer technicians. The two most well-known jobs in the Secret Service are uniformed officer and special agent. All men and women interested in these jobs must meet certain requirements to be considered for recruitment into the Secret Service. They must also go through special training to earn a spot in the agency. Let's take a closer look at what it takes to become a uniformed officer and a special agent.

Becoming an Agent

There are basic requirements that all uniformed officers and special agents must meet. A recruit must have 20/20 vision or vision that can be corrected to 20/20

Secret Service agents learn to sniff out trouble during their training. Here, President George W. Bush watches as members of the Secret Service Uniform Division train bomb-sniffing dogs.

by wearing eyeglasses. Recruits must be physically fit and in excellent health. They must also pass a background check that explores their past. They have to be at least twenty-one years of age and younger than thirty-seven at the time of hiring. The recruits must also be U.S. citizens, have a valid driver's license, and have a high school diploma or equivalent. They must pass a lie detector test, a written exam, and a drug test.

Special agents must have a college degree or three years of law enforcement experience. An advanced college degree in criminal justice, political science, or business administration is the best way agents can advance within the Secret Service.

Training

Newly appointed Secret Service special agents and uniformed officers train at the Federal Law Enforcement Training Center (FLETC) in Glynco, Georgia. FLETC trains people from more than seventy federal agencies. At FLETC, the new agents and

Becoming a Secret Service agent requires a lot of hard work. Doing well in high school and college is the best way to start preparing for a career in the Secret Service.

officers take part in a nine-week training program. The trainees are instructed on subjects such as criminal law and investigative techniques. They learn defensive tactics, how to use firearms, and how to drive a car at high speeds.

After training in Georgia, special agents and uniformed officers move on to different schools for further training.

Special agents move to the Secret Service training headquarters in Beltsville, Maryland. At Beltsville, the agents study how to combat counterfeiting. They also begin their training in physical protection and defense, concentrating on the protection of the president. They learn how to quickly and efficiently gather information. These skills come under the heading of undercover operations. Special agents are trained to spot and stop potential attackers. They become well trained with a variety of firearms. They also learn about the world of financial crimes and how to detect fraud.

After they finish their studies at Beltsville, special agents are sent to a field office for on-the-job training. On-the-job training gives agents the chance to continue learning while beginning their roles as investigators. Experienced agents and managers oversee the progress of the new agents.

Uniformed officers go to the James J. Rowley Training Center in Laurel, Maryland. There they receive eleven weeks of special training.

CLASSIFIED INFORMATION

K-9 Patrols

Using modern technology to sniff out trouble has yet to match the natural abilities of dogs. The Secret Service began using dogs in 1975. The breed of dog the Secret Service uses is called the Belgian Malinois. A Secret Service Uniform Division handler is assigned to work with a dog. The handler and his or her dog become partners, going through twenty weeks of training together. The dogs are taught many things, such as sniffing out explosives and tracking people by their scents.

Chapter Three

A Dangerous Mission

Years of experience have taught the Secret Service to be active and aggressive in the protection of the president. The Secret Service protection division investigates threats against the president's safety every day. Some threats are real. Other threats are hoaxes. Hoaxes are acts meant to fool people. However, no threat is ever taken lightly by the Secret Service.

The Secret Service in Action

To understand how the Secret Service protects the president, let's look at a real case. In March 2000, President Bill Clinton wanted to visit Pakistan during his trip through Asia. However, the Secret Service did not want him to go to Pakistan because they thought it would be too dangerous. The Secret Service believed that there were spies in the Pakistani government's intelligence organization. The Secret Service was concerned that Al Qaeda agents had secretly started working in the organization.

Sometimes the president of the United States disagrees with the security recommendations of the Secret Service. Former president Bill Clinton did just that when he insisted on going to Pakistan during his trip through Asia in March 2000.

Al Qaeda is a group of people who have declared themselves enemies of the United States. Many people believe Al Qaeda is responsible for the terrorist attacks in the United States on September 11, 2001.

The Secret Service advised President Clinton to cancel his trip. The president refused. He wanted to meet with General Pervez Musharraf, the leader of

Pakistan. President Clinton felt it was important to meet with the leader of a nation that owned nuclear weapons. The Secret Service, however, convinced the president to make his visit a short one. President Clinton agreed to stay in Pakistan for only six hours. The Secret Service jumped into action.

Planning for the Worst

The Secret Service had only eighteen days to arrange for the president's security. Normally, preparations take several weeks, to check flight plans and driving routes, and to make a security plan.

The Secret Service did not want to work with the Pakistani government's intelligence groups. They feared the president's movements could be leaked to terrorist organizations. This would leave the president open to attack. With time running out, they made a plan they were confident would work.

President Clinton wanted to meet with Pakistani leader General Pervez Musharraf (shown) to talk about fighting terrorism in and around Pakistan.

The president of the United States flies on *Air Force One*. This Boeing 747 has rooms for the president and an office area for his staff.

Decoy

The Secret Service knows that the best way to protect the president is to keep him far from danger. If that's not possible, they want to fool anyone attempting to harm him. Sometimes the Secret Service pretends the president is in one place when he is actually in another. This is the plan the Secret Service used to protect the president on his visit to Pakistan.

Empty Plane

Air Force One is the president's official airplane. Almost everyone in the world, including terrorists, knows what this huge jet looks like. If the terrorists could shoot down *Air Force One*, then they could hurt or kill the president.

The Secret Service had *Air Force One* land in Islamabad, Pakistan. However, only the plane's pilots and Secret Service agents were onboard. A special agent who looked like the president stepped from the plane. He then went into a waiting limousine. President Clinton actually arrived later in an unmarked plane.

No attack was made on the decoy plane or the look-alike president. However, had there been such an attack, President Clinton would have safely been many miles away.

The Switch

The Secret Service also demanded that the roads be cleared for the president's ride from the airport. Pakistani soldiers lined the roadside as President Clinton's motorcade sped by. Yet this was not the end of the Secret Service's precautions. During the ride, the motorcade stopped beneath an overpass. There, President Clinton switched cars to further trick any would-be assassins. The motorcade continued on to its destination. The president remained safe throughout his visit.

A Job Well Done

The speedy, but successful, planning for the Pakistan visit was not a routine mission for the Secret Service. The Secret Service agents assigned to the Pakistan trip worked long hours to make sure the president would be safe. They also made sure their own agents would remain as safe as possible.

CLASSIFIED INFORMATION

A Dangerous Job

Being a Secret Service agent means risking your life almost every day you are on the job. Over thirty people have died while working as Secret Service agents. Many others have been hurt on the job. Special Agent Tim McCarthy was shot as he tried to protect President Ronald Reagan from would-be assassin John Hinkley, Jr. Agent McCarthy survived his injuries.

Chapter Four

Rising to the Challenge

From the time it began protecting the president, the Secret Service has faced many challenges. The Secret Service has uncovered attempts to assassinate several presidents. Some of these attempts were planned by terrorist groups. Other assassination plans were attempted by individuals angry at the U.S. government. Since it started protecting the president, the Secret Service has failed in its duties only once.

Painful Memories

In November 1963, President John F. Kennedy was assassinated in Dallas, Texas. He was shot while riding in a motorcade. People searched for the reasons the tragedy occurred. They point out that the car in which President Kennedy rode was an open-topped convertible. This made the president an easy target for a gunman. The president's car was also being driven

When shots rang out in Dallas, Texas, on November 22, 1963, Secret Service agents leaped into action. Agent Clinton Hill jumped onto the back of President John F. Kennedy's limousine to shield him from further attack.

very slowly as it made a sharp turn. In addition, the route the president's car took was printed in the local newspapers beforehand. Finally, the route allowed many places for would-be assassins to hide.

President Kennedy's assassination led to changes in the way the Secret Service protects the president. The president no longer drives in open cars. Buildings and motor routes are chosen more carefully. These routes are also searched long before the president's motorcade drives through the area. The Secret Service has learned its lesson well from its one mistake.

CLASSIFIED INFORMATION

The 2002 Winter Olympics security force was made up of:

      2,000 Secret Service agents

      2,400 Utah police officers

      1,100 Federal Bureau of Investigation agents

      2,400 U.S. military personnel

      2,200 fire and emergency workers

After September 11

After September 11, 2001, the threat of terrorist attacks on U.S. soil became a reality. The Secret Service was given more responsibility to combat this different form of criminal activity. The Secret Service was given the authority to oversee the security for major public events, such as the Superbowl.

Going for the Gold

At the 1996 Summer Olympics, in Atlanta, Georgia, a carefully hidden bomb exploded. The explosion killed one woman and injured over a hundred others. To combat future attacks at Olympic games, the Secret Service was put in charge of security of these high-profile international events.

The Secret Service worked with many other law-enforcement agencies in preparation for security at the 2002 Winter Olympics in Salt Lake City, Utah. The Olympics were held in February 2002. The mission of the Secret Service was to protect the 2,600 athletes and 80,000 spectators, who attended the events daily. They also had to protect the 1.8 million people who lived in the Salt Lake City area.

The Secret Service had a winning formula for success at the 2002 Winter Olympics in Utah. The Secret Service worked with other local and federal agencies. Even the U.S. Army was asked to provide soldiers to protect athletes and spectators.

Taking No Chances

The security budget for the 2002 Winter Olympics was over $300 million. Security for an event had never been tighter. The Secret Service ordered aircraft not to fly near places where the Olympic games were held. In fact, only U.S. military jets were allowed to fly in the area. They were patrolling for hostile aircraft. People going to the games were searched with handheld metal detectors. Their bags were also searched. Security cameras were set up to keep an eye on the movements of people in crowds. Sensors were set up to detect chemical and biological weapons.

Secret Service sharpshooters also patrolled the grounds around the Olympic village. The sharpshooters used skis, snowshoes, and snowmobiles to get around. They were equipped with avalanche kits, handcuffs, and special devices for seeing in the dark. The Olympics went on without a problem. The months of security planning paid off. After the Olympics, the U.S. Congress praised the Secret Service and the other law enforcement agencies that had provided protection.

The Future of the Secret Service

Since the beginning of the new century, the Secret Service has found that its job has become tougher to do. Computers make counterfeiting and fraud easier. Terrorists are more dangerous.

However, the Secret Service continues to change with the times. The men and women of the Secret Service work hard to stay ahead of criminals and terrorists. No matter what the threat, the Secret Service will be ready to protect the president and the nation.

The Secret Service will continue to keep watch for threats in the years ahead — no matter where those threats come from.

New Words

assassin someone who commits murder, especially of a leader of a country or group

avalanche a mass of snow and ice moving swiftly down the side of a mountain

counterfeit imitation or fake

decoy someone who draws attention away from someone else

e-crimes crimes committed on the Internet against people or companies that use the Internet

financial crimes crimes involving forging money, harming business computer systems, and stealing money by tricking people

forger someone who makes fake things, such as counterfeit money

New Words

fraud the use of dishonesty to trick or cheat someone

identity theft stealing someone's private identification information to create fake accounts used to make fraudulent purchases

investigate to search or closely examine the details of something, such as a crime

motorcade a group of cars moving along the same route

precautions actions taken beforehand to prevent harm

residence a place, such as a house, where someone lives

sharpshooters people with good shooting skills

For Further Reading

Gaines, Ann Graham. *The U.S. Secret Service*. Philadelphia, PA: Chelsea House, 2001.

January, Brendan. *The Assassination of Abraham Lincoln*. Danbury, CT: Children's Press, 1999.

Jones, Rebecca C. *The President Has Been Shot!: True Stories of the Attacks on Ten U.S. Presidents*. New York, NY: Dutton Children's Books, 1996.

Stein, R. Conrad. *The Assassination of John F. Kennedy*. Danbury, CT: Children's Press, 1993.

Resources

Organization
United States Secret Service
Office of Government Liaison & Public Affairs
950 H Street, Northwest
Suite 8400
Washington, DC 20223
(202) 406-5708

Web Sites
The Official United States Secret Service Web Site
www.secretservice.gov/index.shtml
This official government Web site tells about the Secret Service's history, mission, and overall plan. Find out where field offices are located and how you can apply to become an agent.

Resources

Federal Law Enforcement Training Center

www.fletc.gov/

This Web site has information about the training provided by the Federal Law Enforcement Training Center.

Index

Index

About the Author

Mark Beyer has written more than fifty young adult and children's books. His interest in law enforcement and government has led him to follow the advancement of agencies such as the Secret Service, FBI, CIA, and National Security Agency. He lives outside New York City.